# A PALPABLE PRESENCE

*by*

*William Ruleman*

Published by Feather Books
Shrewsbury, England

Cover Image, *The Wings of Dawn*, acrylic on canvas board by William Ruleman

Cover design by Anne Ruleman Barach

ISBN: 1 84175 071 9

**Number 135 in the Feather Books Poetry Series**

# PREFACE to the 2nd PRINTING

Over a decade has passed since this book was first printed. I
have made only nominal changes to the original. One of my
aims in doing this was to retain a true sense of the way I
thought and wrote when I published these poems twelve years
ago. Another was to show my debt to its initial readers. Let me
explain. When my second book appeared, the year after this
one, I was certain that readers would find it more appealing, for
I was sure that I had progressed as a poet and that the poems in
that second book reflected that progress. I was surprised to
find that this book proved more popular than the second.
Sometimes what a poet might see as progress can be nothing
more than a certain finesse that has little to do with a poem's
vitality, spirit, or effect on readers. Indeed, often readers know
better than the poet! So, although later editions might contain
revisions to these poems—as a means of testing other
approaches and perhaps attracting still other audiences—I am
printing this again, intact except for some minor changes, with
gratitude to those early readers. I am also grateful to the editors
of the following publications, in which several of the poems in
this volume first appeared: *Envoi*, *Parnassus Literary Journal*, *The
Poetry Church*, and *Psychopoetica*.

--William Ruleman
Athens, Tennessee, June 2014

# Contents

## *A PALPABLE PRESENCE*

## THE DISSATISFIED

Expelled from our lawn play, we loitered in forests
far from the glittering blue meadows of oceans,
blind to the cloud-blemished face of blue sky,
till, roaming for decades, we came to a desert,
whose light (one spinning disc of flames)
seemed too harsh to be hoped for as human.

We longed, though, for others, who (like us) were human,
in tune with the fear we had felt in the forest,
swaying in woe over sweat-purchased flames.
Our search led us out in ships on the ocean,
the water there worthless as dust in the desert;
throats parched, we blinked shyly up at the sky,

and one of us dared to address that sky.
The answer it tendered was tantrum-like, human:
rain as it rarely had in the desert
and all too often, deep in damp forests.
Contented, we cut short our days on the ocean;
though weary, our hearts wafted wistful flames

back home as we told our tale to the flames.
They stuttered kindly, the stars in the sky.
We nurtured our old nostalgia for oceans:
surely what reigned there was right-minded, human.
Why waste our lives wandering lost in forests
or slowly dying out in the desert?

The next voyage made all our vague memories a desert.
Mutineers fed our ship's captain to flames.
How fondly we wished to be back in the forest,
away from the eye of the searing sky,
not needing the knowledge that we were human
(a constant onus out on the ocean).

Frustrated, we moved to master the oceans.

We tested weird weapons out in the desert.
We hungered to make Man hardier than human,
consigning the weak to the company of flames
whose ashes vanished in the vacant sky
that none claimed to note from the nearby forest.

What human face now can we find in the sky?
Can oceans tell us? Or what's left of forests?
Might flames again flower some day in the desert?

*Lord, help all us dissatisfied*
*learn your will and be gratified.*
*Help us to find that resting place*
*where, blinded by Son, we see your face.*

# THE LOCAL ÜBERMENSCHEN

In stark and distant towns,
the übermenschen boast,
proclaiming their renown
to huddled, afraid disciples.
No word or food has come
from the world-embracing east
for some time now, but that's
okay: they've got their staples.

Their inner voices urged
them westward, where the sky
was not crowded out by steeples.
No one told them why
or what might be the cost;
and could they not transplant
flora they'd grown to love:
roses, spruces, maples?

True, it was farther than
they had wished for from the coast.
But then, no average man
could even imagine crabapples
like those that they produced.
 "Community" they had lost
might be regained by tugging
no dearth of milk cows' nipples.

When the sun sinks over the crest
of the azure mountain range,
and a gold light of longing stipples
the wheat, our supermen toast
themselves. Their disciples grapple
with vague impulses to wander
despite their elders' frightening
tales of life back yonder.

*Lord, help the local übermenschen
become receptive to dissension,*

*learning the needed humility*
*to make them receptive to you, and free.*

## THE DREARY

Among us always, until the end of time
are those for whom it is always a dreary day,
rain simply dripping down, the sky and clime
a relentless, petty, and drearily cheerless gray.

Life presses in on them somehow, with its
relentless, petty, and drearily cheerless demands:
the unpaid bills, the errands rain like a blitz
on all their hope's ill-plowed and -seeded lands.

And, carefully, they edit out the shame
of longings hazarded hastily in letters home
or notes to themselves, and hallowed be the name
of one who's shown how useless is a poem.

They think it a crime to encourage those who feel.
Against the excited, they temper their wills to steel.

*Lord, help all the dreary*
*learn to become self-leery.*
*Help them enjoy the rich wine of the Son*
*and see how life in Him can be fun.*

# THE HESITANT

Mistakes we make contemn our wish to rush,
yet what for those "who only stand and wait"?
Will Son and reign appear and even a horse
not led to water discover the hidden drink?

The bird in the cage hates the two scot-free in the bush.
In all our haste and fear of being late,
we acquire, then recall that possession is loss
and into the bog of vain self-loathing sink,

for enraged is our caged and lonely thrush,
when what it desired were Love-dove and its mate.
We mull for days on our action's dross
and wish that earlier, we had thought to think.

Since over our lives rains the deafening hush
of doubt, uncertainty, fickle fate,
because stationary stones gather comfy moss,
well, it's nice sometimes just to stand on the brink

of forever and watch the show, instead of one push
and presto, we're *morto*. Why *not* procrastinate?
Oh dear. It's enough to make the unconscious boss,
hands shake and ice cubes clink.

*Lord, help all the hesitant*
*stop living life like a maiden aunt.*
*Help them confront what the future portends*
*and guide them bravely toward their ends.*

## THE SADLY INTUITIVE, WISTFULLY REMORSEFUL

How did we happen to travel this way?
In times of crisis, we heard one voice.
It beckoned; we followed. The question of choice
never occurred to us till the day

we became adults; then freeways, flight patterns
began to tempt us with alternatives.
The voice became imperative.
Its screams in our brains could create migraines.

In an airport bar we'd sit, paralyzed
by fear and feel like hopeless losers
till a beer and a cloud-sailed sky apprised
us that some could get where they wished, aboard cruisers.

Decisions returned to their old voice-driven course.
We dined on our weaknesses, in wistful remorse.

*Lord, help all the wistfully remorseful*
*learn to be more pragmatic, resourceful,*
*making the best of their mood-muddled days*
*without going round in a "voice"-ruled haze.*

**THE INDECISIVE**

Definite doom awaits us soon if we
are blessed. Otherwise, we shall have to wait
fermenting our giddy anxiety
until Decision Day. It's far too late

to return to our days of ignorant bliss
before we knew we were free to make choices.
Too many streets, and too many voices
depressed us, quite frankly. No tell-tale kiss

did we give the accused. A shame, our lack
of the feeling it took for Peter to hack

off Malchus's ear. Instead, procrastination
that masked itself as prudence, discretion.

Safe in our houses now, and robed with our fears,
we're deprived of relieving, saving tears.

*Lord, help all the indecisive*
*unlearn their fretting souls' divisive,*
*crippling ways; and help them try*
*to* live, *aware that they will die.*

# THE ULTRA-SELECTIVE

Unlike so many, these have refused
to admit to at least that measure of failure
that leads some to choose to share their lives
and agree not to need to be always amused.

For accepting others for what they are
and letting them know what you are too—
like being caught blinking in an old snapshot—
is not as exciting as lives like the weather:

Who knows what those cards will be up to next?
They're the authors, say, and life is the text,
except when found late at night, all alone,
dialing old objects of scrutiny on the phone.

*Lord, help all the ultra-selective*
*strive to find a corrective*
*to their hypercritical ways*
*and learn to accept and praise.*

# THE ONES WEARING BLINDERS

The years, they felt, were not entirely wasted:
Whatever bitter gall was served them to drink,
well, only some of it they actually tasted.
As for the rest, they were much too numb
from toil to have much time to think,
much less to brood over all that life had become.

No captive ever suffered a duller affliction
than they who denied themselves the chance to be free;
and if the need for routine had become an addiction,
it came from the wish to avoid the pain
of the unexpected, however benign it might be.
To maintain habits, they felt, was a way to keep sane.

It seldom occurred to them to wonder why:
the answer, they felt, could only come when you die.

*Lord, help all of us wearing blinders*
*acquire multi-angled viewfinders.*
*Help us to look all around us*
*and see sights that delight and astound us.*

# THE DOUBTFUL, PUTTERING IN PURGATORY

Just who is damned and who is blessed still seems
quite arbitrary to us. We've written reams

on the subject and still no abstruse enough solution.
These fires of doubt, we pray, may prove an ablution

of milder, more mundane questioning below. We feel
quite cheated, denied a look at hell.

This "vision" business fails us at times.
We certainly long for less smoke-clouded climes!

If faith is required to get to heaven,
instead of twelve after Judas, there should be eleven,

for to say, with assurance, the Apostles' Creed,
one should not have to see the holes where he bled.

Among our things, we have found an old mustard seed.
Strange we still have it, for we're quite sure we're dead . . .

*Lord, help the doubtful in purgatory*
*find Life in Your higher category.*
*Free them of the tyranny*
*of vexing thought, to find life in Thee.*

## THE NEUROTICS

Pretending that we're happy
in social situations
might make us better people
(more positive, more cheerful)
but how it saps the energy!
requiring some time for recovery
alone in our rooms, like criminals
sensing the cops suspected
how we had altered our stories
to hide the evidence
and have our alibis make sense
and so regain our calm
and the sense that we are not guilty
for something we didn't do,
we're sure of now—or *are* we?

*Lord, help all us neurotics*
*curb our desire for narcotics.*
*Help us, rather, feel the calm*
*induced by Your love's soothing balm.*

# THE WORN-OUT AND LONELY

Far too many, worn out and lonely, idle and watch
old Hollywood movies for sound and company,
while upwardly-mobile types pause to catch
the late night news, striving to be

as quick, informed, and informative as
the commentators who smile at them;
and children of busy or negligent parents
adore old sitcom re-runs and dream

of life with the Cleavers. Retired voyeurs
recline and savor simulated sex in celluloid;
the laid-off trucker, still hooked on speed,
rides six-guns with the best and defers

his life for a while, like all the others,
suspended in time, it seems, like the stars.

*Lord, help us, the worn out and lonely*
*return to the One and Only*
*source of all energy*
*and be what You meant us to be.*

# THE "NOT GOOD ENOUGH," SORRY!

*The World*: Of course, there are some who will never be good.
We don't mean the sour, resentful types
or the evil ones.  We mean the ones
who really endeavor to do their best,
be nice and all of that.  It's just

that a demon or something inside them thwarts
their attempts to be efficient, precise,
blandly confident, and . . . nice.
They don't really *mean* to be annoying
but are so aware that they *might*  be so

that they end up *being* so.  It's true
that stutters, stammers are their stock in trade,
and what they would see as Freudian slips—
yes, they notice things that you and I d-don't
(now, do we?): a disapproving sigh and, of course,

the friendly and homely neighborhood hovel
we've all trained ourselves to ignore.
They might even notice the wink we may give
to others when some day they finally crack
(in their painfully polite way, of course).

*Lord, help all the "not good enough"*
*realize that they're quite up to snuff.*
*In Your all-leveling eyes,*
*all earthlings become the same size.*

*ON THE ROAD TO CALVARY AND BEYOND*

## ONE FELLOW CITIZEN B. C.
## LETS DOWN HIS GUARD
## WHILE HE TALKS TO HIMSELF

We've got our *Pax Romana* at last.
Just one or two hot spots here and there.
But now there's peace, what's left to do?

I check my weight and pulse by the hour,
consult my lucky stars each night,
and never wake in the dark with a fright,
only the moon on my arm white as bone,
plus, well, this hollow feeling inside
that one more drink and a snack won't fill.

Still, *I'm* better off than most.
Take my next-door neighbor for one.
Old soldier come home, he's lost his nerve.
Crazed that hubby won't share her bed,
his wife's gone ape over hearth gods and wines.

How much of this kind of thing will suffice?
Maybe that's not for me to ask.
Still, am I wrong to wish for one last
sacrifice to end it, no questions, no risk
of him not liking us whatever we did?

They tell me a special child shall be born.
To normal parents, like you and me.
You know that I can't help hoping it's mine.

Got a great love life—three concubines.
Then why do I sometimes wish I were dead?

**MARY**

Not knowing what we know,
that one spring afternoon,
you and the mob would view
your baby, now a man

nailed to beams, on display
like a carcass home from the kill,
you lived out the prophecy
of the angel Gabriel,

surely not very glad
to learn that He'd be King
(what mother prefers a god
to ordinary offspring?).

You did what you were told.
But did you sense, in your womb,
that the stone door would be rolled
on the third day from his tomb?

**THE WISE MEN**

We bring to him
no greater gift
than the sap men tapped
upon hacking the bark
of living trees:
a resin that oozed
from wooden wounds,
congealed through time
into fragrant globs
men nicknamed "tears,"
these redolent blobs
of frankincense, myrrh.

No greater gifts
than these have we,
plus gold for show--
yet what do *we* know?
Myrrh is superb
for cosmetics, perfumes,
and frankincense
may help heal wounds . . .
No greater gifts
to bring have we:
*tears to heal wounds,*
*each from a bleeding tree.*

Our credentials stunning,
we nonetheless bow
to the helpless, uncunning
babe in the hay.
We're sunburned and foolish.
Friends, what have we done?
Still, our sources inform us
this child is the one.
O may he not mind
what little we give,
the best we can offer,
the best the world has:

tears to heal wounds,
each from a bleeding tree.

**THE CRUCIFIERS**

We killed "God's Son" this afternoon
(some would say by mistake)
others, out of resentment over
changes that he would have us make

in our self-contained and fretful lives.
The funny thing is, he forgave us for it--
an act that drove some insane
for the sheer lack of logic in it.

By evening the show was over.
Some lingered near the scene
as over a job doubtfully done,
but most sought suitable shelter,

confiding their doubt to none
although quite willing to offer by phone
the scoop on what others wore
and who stayed distastefully late.

## IN EASTER SEASON

Against grey and umber thickets of branches that seem
the winter's ashes, a wild Adam's unhappy maze,
a wicked world's answer to its doubt-ridden days;
against a mist like that within a dream,

and with a clarity that seems unreal,
like objects viewed but unheard, through a windowpane,
gold buds and emerald leaves sing again of our pain
in re-learning, through the risen Son's warmth, how to feel.

As dogwoods madly foam forth their milky froth,
as redbuds spray and spew their vintage rosé,
scattered, lake-like sky-blue puddles display
the heavens' image, mirrored on the earth.

*SOME EARLY AND LATER SAINTS*

**PROLOGUE**

I see them rising above the dust of the ages,
cool in the amber and ruby and blue of stained glass,
or overflowing the font of Butler's pages,
but ever persecuted: a mass
of figures tortured, burned, crucified,
beheaded, chewed up, mutilated, bruised, and battered
to death, or starved, and that's how many died.
They lived when professing the Christian faith really mattered:

Saint Lucy, felled by a sword thrust into her throat—
just one of thousands I happen upon by chance.
And someone named Leger, who had his eyes put out . . .
Well, nothing merry in old Saint Vitus's dance.
From him I turn, at random, to Maximus,
who could make old Constans II fume and cuss:

flogged, relieved of his tongue and right hand,
he died soon after, just an "old guy" of eighty or so.
Yes, little about their lives was very bland.
Those early saints, it seems, were ever on the go.
While some *invited* suffering, true,
they did what Jesus would have done,
and set a standard—a stern one—for me and you.
True, there are many ways the Kingdom can be won:
Quiet service, not violent sacrifice,
being gentle, patient, tending to the sick and needy;
yet saints are more than simply "nice."
I'd like to honor them all, but won't be greedy,
and so present a few poems in commemoration
of some who suffered for our salvation.

## THOMAS

You're like so many of us,
prepared to die for your faith
one day without a fuss,
the next demanding "the truth."

How doubt can make us suffer,
yet faith's so hard to sustain!
And as to salt's true flavor,
won't it dilute in a rain?

Thomas, you weren't happy
until you touched the wounds.
Today, we see you as lucky:
a Savior, right there on the grounds!

Like all good Platonists,
I've deemed my body a prison.
And yet, those nail-pocked wrists
belonged to a Body, risen.

# AGATHA



*invoked against breast diseases*

Lovely, rich, and also good,
you'd vowed to live in chastity.
Quintian had other plans
for all that cash and purity
but somehow never understood
your unconditional loyalty
to a higher cause than his lust.
His ready matron did her best
to lure you toward salacious sin;
and when he saw she couldn't win,
at first, he merely had you slapped,
but then, when you re-affirmed your faith,
he called you forth and had you strapped
and stretched upon a wooden horse,
tipped your virgin flesh with hooks,
ordered both your breasts hacked off,
then ordered you rolled over burning coals.

When did the ghost of Peter come down?
He healed your hurts, but not the souls
of Quintian and Co., of that I am sure,
for an earthquake rumbled and shook the town,
crushing Quintian's torturer;
and Quintian fled for his life, terrified.
Thanking God for His mercy, you died.

Since then, you have been the patron saint
of all who earn their bread founding bells.
A strange connection, except when you think
of bells and breasts, then you see the link.

May your breasts, like bells, toll their complaint
with those of us in private hells
of bodily comfort; please, may they ring
for those who suffer indignities
to their womanhood and beauty today;

severed breasts, ring, and help us pray
that they may be freed of their agonies
and find, in their pain, a reason to sing.

**BLAISE**

Alone in his cave on Mount Argeus, he prays.
Both man and beast approach him to be healed.
The animals wait until his lips are sealed
before they apprise him of their disease.

Agricola sends his hunters to the woods
to flush out sport for his arena games.
Aghast are the men to see how well Blaise tames
lions, tigers, bears, and wolves with mere words.

One with such power has to be held in check.
He's thrown into prison, threatened, and begged to cease
his "foolishness," yet, with his usual peace,
he keeps on healing the sinful, unhappy, and sick.

Seeking him silenced, they hurl him into the drink.
He shocks them all by walking like Christ on the waves
and asks them to prove the worth of the gods they praise
by joining him. They do, but of course, they sink.

An angel commands him to walk back to the shore,
there to accept his appointed martyrdom.
He watches those who hate and fear him come,
grab and dash him to the dirt and swear,

wrench back his locks, hack right through his neck,
and watch the head drop, perhaps wobbling as it settles,
with a sunbathed marble peace that no doubt nettles
them, gaping at one who healed for Jesus' sake.

## BARBARA

Hardly "Christian-friendly,"
your appointed time and place.
In your native Nicodemia,
Maxinimus of Thrace
amused himself in his reign
with a daily amphora of wine
and shattering horses' jaws
with single blows of his fist.

Your daddy, Dioscurus,
placed you in a palace
topped by a massive tower
and margined by marvelous gardens
wherein you parried with poets
and other learned men
whose wisdom made you see
the blatant absurdity
of worshipping many Gods.

You hurled pagan busts from the tower,
carved crosses upon the walls,
thus irritating your father,
who decided that you must die.
After you fled to the mountains,
he nonetheless overtook you,
dragging you home by the hair
and handing you over to Marcian,
Maxinimus' assistant,
who had you beaten with rods,
torn with iron hooks,
until kind Father saw fit
to put an end to it all
by chopping off your head.

Now you're invoked against sudden death
and final impenitence.
For us, you drew your final breath
and in Heaven find your recompense.

## CECILIA

*(as later recounted by the Roman prefect, Almachius,
 to a private gathering of friends)*

Good family, good contacts—just can't understand.
She wished to remain a virgin . . . for *God?*
Her old man made her marry, though.
Not a bad sort, her hubby: Valerian his name.
She duped the poor sod into falling for
some tale about her "guardian angel."
To see it, he had to be "baptized." Sheesh!
The next thing you know, man, he and his bro
are trying to bury *Christians*. Jesus!
They left us no choice but decap.

Then the bitch had the gall to bury *them*—
had them "interred" at her "villa."
Guys, what's a prefect to do?
We tried something gentle at first:
suffocation by steam in her bath.
Darned if it wouldn't take.
So had to resort to dull old decap.

Get a load of this item in "Round About Town":
"Her body, sans head, remains on display
in its cypress coffin at Trastevere,
robed in its cloth of gold.
Visiting hours are from . . ."
This is too much. I can't go on.
Fellas, pour me another.

## GEORGE

Martyred at Lydda in Palestine
before the accession of Constantine—
that alone do we know. More famous, of course,
the tale of you galloping off on your horse
to slay the dragon scaring that village,
breathing fire, creating pillage,
demanding two sheep a day to appease it,
though when sheep were scarce, all that could please it
were maidens, drawn from the town by lot.
Woe seemed sure as you came trot-
ting forth, the lot fallen to the daughter of the king.
Love made your life seem a paltry thing.
You killed the beast with one sting of your lance.
Before the town grew dizzy with dance,
you urged them to shun their pagan ways.
They did. The king replied with his praise,
his daughter's hand and a stash to boot.
Declining the girl, you took the loot
to give to the poor. Rejecting fame
and ease, you rode toward martyrdom.

# TO IGNATIUS OF ANTIOCH
# AND ALL THE EARLY MARTYRS

It's certain your readiness to suffer had
effect on Christians and pagans both in time.
You begged your brethren to let beasts shed your blood,
to mill your flesh—"the wheat of the Lord"—to become
the host: the "immaculate bread of Christ."
Because of you, cruelty tended to lose its charm.
Admiring the lions as they thrashed about in the dust
your mangled limbs as though you felt no harm
grew dull as watching a child tear up a doll.
Aghast at your resolute faith and passivity,
how many quivered in helpless rage—a hell
of power thwarted, until serenity
could be achieved only by a grudging acceptance?
Your agony paved the way for our convenience.

*We thank you, Ignatius, and all*
*the early martyrs like you*
*for your  irresistible faith*
*that has made our own faith much easier.*
*We pray for those in darker,*
*barbaric places on earth*
*who suffer even today.*

*Help us summon the strength,*
*the sense of necessity,*
*to help them in their need*
*for the Church's and Jesus' sake.*

# WHERE ARE WE NOW, AND WHERE ARE WE GOING?

# NEW YEAR'S, 2001

The Christmas season almost ended,
we write to friends who sent us cards
without our writing, first, to them.
Our faces flushed, our bellies distended,
we send them all our kind regards
and maybe (faintly) hum a hymn

inspired by the chimes at the corner church
that keep on praising while we've gone on
to taking back unwanted gifts
to the malls, afraid to be left in the lurch
by an age whose speed won't leave us alone
with ourselves; we're afraid, as the silent sand sifts

down the glass? Oh no, our digital clocks
convey the passing of time in a blink,
and we find ourselves a century older
without enough gained from our bonds and stocks,
while the diehards down another neat drink,
and the fretful seek in vain a soft shoulder.

Where's the "sweet babe in the hay" in all this?
He little foresaw the death *He* would die.
O Child of our fondest hopes and dreams,
help us see how, so neatly, we've yet gone amiss.
Drown our petty fears in that infant's cry
which points to healing, Son-graced beams.

## ONE RECENT SUMMER

A jet makes its home in a swamp.
A gun digs an early grave.
Someone learns how to save,
fifty skulls are unearthed at a camp.

Some more of the ozone melts.
Computers catch a new virus.
Somewhere, a new cult of Osiris.
More bombing by angry Celts.

Thousands, somewhere, are weeping.
*Yet the crime rate's on the decrease.*
Will wonders never cease?
A mood of malaise goes creeping

over the lands, the oceans,
underground, in the airwaves . . .
It's summer, and everyone craves
the latest sunscreen lotions.

The First Lady finds a soothsayer.
A hurricane rips off a coast.
Economy's better for most,
and who is kneeling in prayer?

# A SECOND COMING

I saw Jesus again today. He drove up in
the new silver Mercedes, dressed
in that pin-striped Brooks Brothers suit,
sitting next to J. I.,
the head of p. r. for our firm.

I felt we'd set him up right.
The only thing wrong
was the hair and the beard. I waited till
we'd had a few Scotch and Perriers
till I mentioned my reservations.
Flower children. Peace. Those
went out in the Sixties. Slightly
unshaven, maybe—but not a full bush.

He said he would have to think about it,
so I know he'll give in, much as he has
with everything else. I mean,
who'd listen to him the way he was,
in that crazy cloak and flip-flops?
He'll get so much better coverage now,
with the Last Supper live by satellite
from Maxim's, and a stunt man doing
the Crucifixion bit, with an extra or two
for the Tomb scene, though we've taken out
a huge policy, just in case some sick
publicity hound decides to do him in personally.

All of this, a second time around,
he objected violently to at first,
but when he saw that we were right,
that no one would ever believe it *at all*
if he didn't let us handle it *our* way,
then he waxed philosophical about it—
got even a little indifferent—which made
J. I. and the rest of us panic a little,
thinking he might not go through with it.
I mean, he seems so passive, so apathetic,

so now we're just trying to humor him along—
trying to make him see reason.
We're quite willing to negotiate.
He can't have given up on us.
We've certainly not given up on *him*.

# THE FASHION SLAVES EXPLAIN
# THEIR DISFAVOR

It's not that we find you boring.
It's just that we might find more to say
at cocktail parties and church
if only you wrote a sexy screenplay
or embezzled some corporate funds—
something, at least, not worth ignoring
so you won't be left in the lurch
or ridiculed by your best friends.

It's not that we no longer like you,
for nothing could ever equal
the interest we take in your life
in gauging your chance for survival
in this cutthroat climate we live in.
We hate what we put you—all of us—through.
But we must keep causing grief:
How else could we be forgiven?

# A DIFFICULT STRANGER

The folks at church got quiet when
they heard him say he was poor;
they let him speak his peace and then
an usher showed him the door.

The folks at church got nervous when
he came next week as before;
they eyed one another (who let him in?)
and wondered what was in store.

The folks at church got *more* nervous when
he coughed and took the floor:
"If anyone here is free of sin,
well, I'm an apple core."

The folks at church got fed up when
the priest and the deacon bore
the bread and wine to this bum, who dropped ten
measly pennies into the plate. They were sore.

The folks in church got touchy when
he spoke fondly of Galilee's shore.
They changed the topic to who would win
the next game, and which stars would score.

The folks at church got testy when
he said his best friend was a whore:
some tramp named Mary Magdalene . . .
This guy was really a boor!

The folks at church got angry when
he said not to think of war—
not even against those truly *mad* men
who thrive on blood and gore!

The folks at church got murderous when
he kept citing Biblical lore
and telling them all that he was their friend;

yes, "setting him free" was a chore.

The folks at church got sheepish when
their arms and legs grew sore:
a burden, wielding that heavy coffin
while noting what everyone wore.

## YOU'VE PLENTY OF TIME, DON'T WORRY!

The average human life span now gives ample time
in which to stray, then mend our ways;
we're all adults, our friends and we, and none will mind
when our behavior deviates
somewhat from the norm; they may even like you a whole lot
more
for giving them something to talk about:
a crime or affair they never, *ever*, in their lives would have dared
to conceive or begin, the concept of sin
too strongly ingrained in them—somehow—from childhood
days
or when, or where? It's not really clear,
but all at once, you're seen as unique for having done
what they had always dreamed of, but none
had the guts to do, like telling the boss off or getting up
in church and shouting a four-letter word.

For acts such as these we may often find we're admired, if
alone,
but, of course, we have years in which to atone.

## A LULL IN THE BATTLE

It's nearing midnight. Slowly the world's winding down.
A car droned past a moment ago, and rain-
drops tap the metal porch roof. I guess I'm sane,
and sane, for now, this sleepy little town
where a few dogs bark, and night is cloaked in a gown
of fog, and crickets chime, and surely no pain
is felt by anyone. Raising Cain
on a Sunday night is not our style. We frown
on Sabbath sensations. But come tomorrow morn,
we rev up our engines again, resume the race
for the fruit that will make us the apple of His eye.
All of our songs, the mad sun, and our glances warn
ourselves and others not to slacken our pace.
We know that some will fly, and some will die,
and none of us ever stops to question why.

## INDEED, "WHAT DOES IT PROFIT"?

Sometimes, in the drive for brutal honesty,
we may overlook the truth, which often may shy
away from words, as cruel to the budding tree
of love as blistering noonday sun in July.
Acidic words that etch into one's soul
or eat, like a brown recluse's juice, through flesh,
critique that makes of starry-eyed hope a black hole
and the wheat of promise we've sown too shriveled to thresh.
We do our damnedest, don't we, to make ourselves heard,
and biting wit or caustic scorn suffice
to get the attention, in lieu of a gentler word.
It's true that one can't get ahead just by being "nice."
But in gaining the world we may lose what is real,
numbing our delicate power to love and feel.

## HE DREAMS OF "DESTRUCTION
THAT WASTETH AT NOONDAY"

(July 2000)

I feel that we're fast approaching a darker time.
What happened to decency, good taste, and manners?
Too many gripe groups, flashing their venom-stained banners.
And poets are scorned when they aim for a "lofty rhyme."
To talk of Beauty might as well be a crime.
Alert to tender sentiments, cynical scanners
delete the gentle for manic media planners:
into the wee hours shines their status lights' lime.
Some days I dream that the night has already come;
at noon I blink and stumble, as if in the dark.
I doze, in a daze, though at midnight I stare, awake,
my heart in sync with the "future's frenzied drum."
I know my "prophecy" isn't worth a quark,
and yet keep sensing that something is going to break.

## A REAL PROBLEM

Pretending not to see
a casual acquaintance
passing at some distance;
feigning not to be
who you undoubtedly are—
oh, why do you do that, my body?
Your ways can be perfectly shoddy,
totally at war

with everything Jesus said:
"Love thy neighbor" especially,
and so the spirit's unfed
because of what we did
or did not do or say
earlier in the day,
or else it finds itself thwarted
because of hopes we'd aborted
also earlier in the day.

A sudden troubling thought:
everyone we meet
no matter how tangential
to our own life plan, is still
significant somehow:
so the waitress you were rude to
and even disdained to tip;
the student you refused
to give any outside help to;
the beggar you brushed off;
the patient you carelessly,
inaccurately diagnosed;
the stranger you saw on the street
and passed without a smile to—
are nonetheless part of your life
and together comprise a part
of your pilgrimage through this world.

# A MIDSUMMER PRAYER

Submitting daily—no, minute by minute—to sin;
immersed in it as in this midsummer heat;
my soul like the screeching cicadas cries out
for release from the sweating, persistent friction
of body and soul that struggle to act as one.
Day brings routine, glib talk, and hiding; but night
and silence re-light my vexing refrain:
"I'll change tomorrow," I say, then think: "You will not,"
till, aided by prayer, fatigue, and a bath, I ask
my Savior: "Forgive me all my petty transgressions,
especially my wish to make a fetish of
my suffering. Forgive me my doubt that shies from risk,
my flight from the heat of the day, decisions.
Then help me to find the cool shade of your Love."

**A REQUEST FOR REFINEMENT**

So many of us are greedy for heaven:
we seek to find it on earth,
fighting day by day to get even
with a fate that has dealt us dearth.
The gods of power, mammon, prestige,
fashions, hype, the Net, tv—
all may send us into a rage
when they ensnare us. We're only free
when fixing our gaze on eternity,
moving as in a dance through this world
of bosoms and billfolds and bacon and bores . . .
But what to do with all our fears
that our yearning for Eden will go unfulfilled?
O that our spirits may be refined
in fires that cleanse the earth-clinging mind!

## AFTER THE BREAKDOWN:
## A BENEDICTION

No more let Mind extol its vain
insistence on Activity,
or martyred Psyche welcome Pain,
or Feeling show passivity
toward Will's impressive reign.

No more let Heart's timidity
suffer Super-ego's cane,
or Reason force Love to stammer and cry
because she cannot be sane.

*A PALPABLE PRESENCE*

# "LET THE NEEDS OF THE DAY BE SUFFICIENT"

I may be in debt, but my credit is good.
I've plenty to eat and drink, and in winter, I'm warm.
I'm downright hot in summer; but that's no harm:
Sweating is something since Adam we've all understood.
The world of work—well, it's hardly a "sacred wood."
True, "playing the market" can have its elusive charm.
Just make your million and leave that blasted farm!
Or so the sages say. As if everyone could.
But carnal life can only savor so much.
A cabin can be as cozy as a palace;
fried cod with chips, as tasty as caviar;
a Styrofoam cup, as supple to the touch
as a priceless, savagely-coveted golden chalice
to those who know what fragile vessels we are.

# EVEN UNTIL THE END

*(in memory of Blanche Melton Haney)*

And what can I say of you after
that final stroke, except that, perhaps,
in losing most of your tongue for the speech
you had used for communion with us all your life,
you were venturing toward another realm
where words of our ilk would no longer do?

Till the end one phrase never left you, however.
Despite legs like sticks, and shriveled paps,
and food-caked claws with trembling reach,
and a stare as incisive at times as a knife;
despite a fear that would overwhelm
you at moments, as if some querulous voodoo

and you had been matched, to a sorceress's laughter;
despite my lack of appropriate psychic maps
to trace the path of your wants in that screech
that articulated your inner strife;
you yet steered through your storm, strong at the helm,
able even to the end to manage "I love you."

# A CONDEMNED SOUL ACQUIRING FAITH

"Evening now. The western sky
suffused with pink above the trees:
pines smoky green, and mushrooming oaks
as black and liquid as melting tar.

I stand alone and wish to die.
The scene before me gives no peace.
At dawn I'll feel death's rope, which chokes.
Good God, please tell me where you are."

"My son, I'm here," a voice inside
his mind replies, though it sounds too like
a human voice, so he starts to scowl.
It's faint and almost matter-of-fact,

not bullying, or meant to deride
or make him angry at someone, and strike
as did the voice that ran him afoul,
the voice that always made him act.

He waits for commands, but hears nothing more.
He scowls again, then strains to hear
the voice again. The effort this takes
absorbs him completely. Instead of *doing*,

his task is now to become a bore
to himself, embracing the silence that fear
forbade him once to hear. Mistakes
are the past. Death's a lover, wooing.

## A WINTER HYMN

Here, in a mist-cloaked winter wood,
rain-blackened branches brittle, austere,
a redbird sings—of me, unaware
and not having heard of something called God

yet trilling, alone, for no good reason
that I can see—I, one who demands
justifications, means with clear ends,
renewal of proof that Christ has arisen.

My doubt is the dread that I shall die.
My desire? To remain preserved, intact,
to clutter all darkness and mystery with fact,
to answer, with logic, the question *why?*

The bird, I'm sure, knows no such questions,
its song the voice of certainty.
Its hue, the red of mortality,
asserts much more than abstract suggestions.

My own hue today feels bland, rather beige,
or as dishwater-grey as the dull day itself,
my soul numb within, or hollowed in half,
dim-witted, a tree trunk that none can budge

till the redbird's silver song reminds me
how brief is grief, how dearthful death,
and summons spring, hence further life,
the seasons' cycle that echoes eternity.

## "WHEN I WAS A CHILD . . .
I THOUGHT LIKE A CHILD . . ."

As boys, we loved our games of war
that left us with never so much as a scar . . .
I take that back, for *we'd* throw rocks,
and one struck me on the noggin once.
I was stunned, and I bled, but the rage was such
that the pain was less than the threat that mocks
the self, hard as flint, and blind to the chance
that love can provide other ways to touch.

## THE CHILD IS FATHER TO LIGHT AND LACK OF CONCENTRATION AT WORK

(November 1986)

"A man's born twice,"
Frieda Lawrence said:
once of his mother,
once of his wife.
I say *thrice*:
once of his child,
whose coming, rather
like nothing in life
or history, unless
like that of Christ,
blinds him to all
but the miracle
of life from dust,
shining down
on his petty plans,
paling each
with a fine kind of light,
making each less
than dust in his sight.

## SOME LINES IN LIGHT OF MORE FAMOUS ONES
## FROM *MACBETH*
(Fall 1988)

"Out, out—!" my two-year-old daughter cries
at twilight, demanding more outdoor play,
though lately she's been disturbed by her shadow's
careless yet resolute tyranny,

moved to tears by her failure to shun
one means by which to roughly gauge
life's rise and fall, each age-caged stage.
"Out, out, brief . . . " Well, *you* know the lines.

Someday so may she, though I've steadfast (if giddy)
hope even then she will be as ready
to move toward the Light, despite
the *light* of things; though critics might

make "*moth*-to-light" jokes, let her endeavor
to show that Light, not shadow, rules forever.

# LINES COMPOSED IN MID-MARCH

After the rain, a pinkish light
suffuses the straw I've strewn upon
my lawn, where I've sown fresh seed.
Daffodils in their chocolate beds
radiate with such a light
they seem as if from another planet,
while our lone forsythia's tentacles wave
their lemon stars like fronds underwater . . .

Moved by the miracle of this sight,
I find my wintry fear and gloom gone.
Vanished, at least for the moment, my need
for shuffling *buts*, *althoughs*, *insteads*.
Freed of a dread as heavy as granite,
I feel again all Heaven gives
to us via Earth, His own dear daughter.

# THOUGHTS IN MAY

I seek the warmth of the Son
to burn away my sin;
May has come again,
and love and life seem one
in the life I see all around.

So supple and green each leaf,
so pleasant every sound,
so rich the scented air
with scent of honeyed flower,
so dizzying the grief
that mourns each passing hour.

O youth, that sinks its teeth
into its own keen flesh
and draws blood rich and fresh,
loving life to death;

O age, that tastes the breeze
like an old dog sniffing a scent,
recalling bygone days
and wondering what they meant;

this May the summer is beckoning;
the prisoner yearns for release;
Death delays its reckoning
for some, for some gives peace.

Do not neglect this day;
the sun is shining for you.
Do not forget to pray
Heaven's sky will be this blue.

## "I SEE THE CHILDREN SPORT UPON THE SHORE"

I long for the young I have loved who will come here no more
to welter with us in this, our wave-wearied world.
Perhaps they wait for us on some distant shore.

I watch in wait for the tender who've gone before.
I ache to see them again, their sails unfurled.
I long for the young I have loved who will come here no more.

A worm of worry has corkscrewed my heart to its core.
I've chafed and wondered where their souls have been hurled.
Perhaps they wait for us on some distant shore.

The dreams they dared may have died; forgotten, the score
of a game they once won; but, recalling hair thick and curled,
I long for the young I have loved who will come here no more.

Their deeds are dust, casualties in Time's tedious war.
And yet his pale green eyes, that fiery tress she twirled—.
I long for the young I have loved who will come here no more.

They're crumbled cake . . . I wonder what it's all for,
this flimsy life so richly boyed and girled.
I long for the young I have loved who will come here no more.
I trust that they wait for us on eternity's shore.

# WHAT SHALL REMAIN

If "golden lads and girls all must
as chimney sweepers, come to dust,"
the question is how our knowing this
might change the way we live our lives.
The prospect of eternal bliss
can help the one who thinks and strives

to live with an eye that looks past death,
to ponder, indeed, that every breath
one takes leads to life beyond the grave,
so striving for earthly permanence
cannot provide the means to save
us from losing a grip on earthly existence.

Inside our souls, as in a tree bole's rings,
are etched the lines of bygone springs,
as well as the scars of grief.
Yet scars, in time, decay, then disappear.
Let no grim scars remain, but Love;
When all else fades, let Love be here.

## ABOUT THE AUTHOR

William Ruleman teaches in the Department of English and Modern Languages at Tennessee Wesleyan College in Athens, Tennessee. He received his Ph.D. from the University of Mississippi in 1994. His article *W.H. Auden's Search for a Faith* and second book of poems, *Profane and Sacred Loves* (2002) have also been published by Feather Books. His translations of poems from Rilke's *Neue Gedichte* (1907) appeared from Will Hall Books in 2003, and his translations of early stories and novellas of Stefan Zweig appeared from Ariadne Press in 2010. This is the second printing of *A Palpable Presence*, which was originally published in 2001.